Preparing Your Kitchen!

The Year-Round Meal Planner for Families

@ Journals and Notebooks

@ *Journals & Notebooks*

January

thinkpositive ● exercise daily
eat healthy ● dance more
Love often ● be happy

	Breakfast	Lunch	Dinner
Date : **Monday**			
Date : **Tuesday**			
Date : **Wednesday**			
Date : **Thursday**			
Date : **Friday**			
Saturday			
Date : **Sunday**			

thinkpositive ● exercise daily
eat healthy ● dance more
Love often ● be happy

	Breakfast	Lunch	Dinner
Date : **Monday**			
Date : **Tuesday**			
Date : **Wednesday**			
Date : **Thursday**			
Date : **Friday**			
Saturday			
Date : **Sunday**			

thinkpositive ● exercise daily
eat healthy ● dance more
Love often ● be happy

	Breakfast	Lunch	Dinner
Date : **Monday**			
Date : **Tuesday**			
Date : **Wednesday**			
Date : **Thursday**			
Date : **Friday**			
Saturday			
Date : **Sunday**			

thinkpositive ● exercise daily
eat healthy ● dance more
Love often ● be happy

	Breakfast	Lunch	Dinner
Date : **Monday**			
Date : **Tuesday**			
Date : **Wednesday**			
Date : **Thursday**			
Date : **Friday**			
Saturday			
Date : **Sunday**			

thinkpositive ● exercise daily
eat healthy ● dance more
Love often ● be happy

Notes:

Things to Buy:

thinkpositive ● exercise daily
eat healthy ● dance more
Love often ● be happy

Meal Planner

Meal Planner

Be Healthy

thinkpositive ● exercise daily
eat healthy ● dance more
Love often ● be happy

Meal Planner

	Breakfast	Lunch	Dinner
Date : **Monday**			
Date : **Tuesday**			
Date : **Wednesday**			
Date : **Thursday**			
Date : **Friday**			
  Saturday			
Date : **Sunday**			

thinkpositive ● exercise daily
eat healthy ● dance more
Love often ● be happy

	Breakfast	Lunch	Dinner
Date : **Monday**			
Date : **Tuesday**			
Date : **Wednesday**			
Date : **Thursday**			
Date : **Friday**			
Saturday			
Date : **Sunday**			

thinkpositive ● exercise daily
eat healthy ● dance more
Love often ● be happy

	Breakfast	Lunch	Dinner
Date : **Monday**			
Date : **Tuesday**			
Date : **Wednesday**			
Date : **Thursday**			
Date : **Friday**			
Saturday			
Date : **Sunday**			

thinkpositive ● exercise daily
eat healthy ● dance more
Love often ● be happy

	Breakfast	Lunch	Dinner
Date : **Monday**			
Date : **Tuesday**			
Date : **Wednesday**			
Date : **Thursday**			
Date : **Friday**			
Saturday			
Date : **Sunday**			

thinkpositive ● exercise daily
eat healthy ● dance more
Love often ● be happy

Notes:

Things
to Buy:

thinkpositive ● exercise daily
eat healthy ● dance more
Love often ● be happy

Meal Planner

Meal Planner

March

thinkpositive ● exercise daily
eat healthy ● dance more
Love often ● be happy

	Breakfast	Lunch	Dinner
Date : **Monday**			
Date : **Tuesday**			
Date : **Wednesday**			
Date : **Thursday**			
Date : **Friday**			
Saturday			
Date : **Sunday**			

thinkpositive ● exercise daily
eat healthy ● dance more
Love often ● be happy

	Breakfast	Lunch	Dinner
Date : **Monday**			
Date : **Tuesday**			
Date : **Wednesday**			
Date : **Thursday**			
Date : **Friday**			
  Saturday			
Date : **Sunday**			

thinkpositive ● exercise daily
eat healthy ● dance more
Love often ● be happy

Meal Planner

	Breakfast	Lunch	Dinner
Date : **Monday**			
Date : **Tuesday**			
Date : **Wednesday**			
Date : **Thursday**			
Date : **Friday**			
Saturday			
Date : **Sunday**			

thinkpositive ● exercise daily
eat healthy ● dance more
Love often ● be happy

	Breakfast	Lunch	Dinner
Date : **Monday**			
Date : **Tuesday**			
Date : **Wednesday**			
Date : **Thursday**			
Date : **Friday**			
Saturday			
Date : **Sunday**			

thinkpositive ● exercise daily
eat healthy ● dance more
Love often ● be happy

Notes:

Things to Buy:

thinkpositive ● exercise daily
eat healthy ● dance more
Love often ● be happy

Meal Planner

Meal Planner

April

thinkpositive ● exercise daily
eat healthy ● dance more
Love often ● be happy

	Breakfast	Lunch	Dinner
Date : **Monday**			
Date : **Tuesday**			
Date : **Wednesday**			
Date : **Thursday**			
Date : **Friday**			
Saturday			
Date : **Sunday**			

thinkpositive ● exercise daily
eat healthy ● dance more
Love often ● be happy

	Breakfast	Lunch	Dinner
Date : **Monday**			
Date : **Tuesday**			
Date : **Wednesday**			
Date : **Thursday**			
Date : **Friday**			
Saturday			
Date : **Sunday**			

thinkpositive ● exercise daily
eat healthy ● dance more
Love often ● be happy

	Breakfast	Lunch	Dinner
Date : **Monday**			
Date : **Tuesday**			
Date : **Wednesday**			
Date : **Thursday**			
Date : **Friday**			
Saturday			
Date : **Sunday**			

thinkpositive ● exercise daily
eat healthy ● dance more
Love often ● be happy

	Breakfast	Lunch	Dinner
Date : **Monday**			
Date : **Tuesday**			
Date : **Wednesday**			
Date : **Thursday**			
Date : **Friday**			
Saturday			
Date : **Sunday**			

thinkpositive ● exercise daily
eat healthy ● dance more
Love often ● be happy

Meal Planner

Notes:

Things to Buy:

thinkpositive ● exercise daily
eat healthy ● dance more
Love often ● be happy

Meal Planner

Meal Planner

think positive ● exercise daily
eat healthy ● dance more
Love often ● be happy

	Breakfast	Lunch	Dinner
Date : **Monday**			
Date : **Tuesday**			
Date : **Wednesday**			
Date : **Thursday**			
Date : **Friday**			
Saturday			
Date : **Sunday**			

thinkpositive ● exercise daily
eat healthy ● dance more
Love often ● be happy

	Breakfast	Lunch	Dinner
Date : **Monday**			
Date : **Tuesday**			
Date : **Wednesday**			
Date : **Thursday**			
Date : **Friday**			
Saturday			
Date : **Sunday**			

thinkpositive ● exercise daily
eat healthy ● dance more
Love often ● be happy

	Breakfast	Lunch	Dinner
Date : **Monday**			
Date : **Tuesday**			
Date : **Wednesday**			
Date : **Thursday**			
Date : **Friday**			
Saturday			
Date : **Sunday**			

thinkpositive ● exercise daily
eat healthy ● dance more
Love often ● be happy

	Breakfast	Lunch	Dinner
Date : **Monday**			
Date : **Tuesday**			
Date : **Wednesday**			
Date : **Thursday**			
Date : **Friday**			
Saturday			
Date : **Sunday**			

thinkpositive ● exercise daily
eat healthy ● dance more
Love often ● be happy

Notes:

Things to Buy:

thinkpositive ● exercise daily
eat healthy ● dance more
Love often ● be happy

Meal Planner

thinkpositive ● exercise daily
eat healthy ● dance more
Love often ● be happy

Meal Planner

thinkpositive ● exercise daily
eat healthy ● dance more
Love often ● be happy

	Breakfast	Lunch	Dinner
Date : **Monday**			
Date : **Tuesday**			
Date : **Wednesday**			
Date : **Thursday**			
Date : **Friday**			
Saturday			
Date : **Sunday**			

thinkpositive ● exercise daily
eat healthy ● dance more
Love often ● be happy

	Breakfast	Lunch	Dinner
Date : **Monday**			
Date : **Tuesday**			
Date : **Wednesday**			
Date : **Thursday**			
Date : **Friday**			
Saturday			
Date : **Sunday**			

thinkpositive ● exercise daily
eat healthy ● dance more
Love often ● be happy

	Breakfast	Lunch	Dinner
Date : **Monday**			
Date : **Tuesday**			
Date : **Wednesday**			
Date : **Thursday**			
Date : **Friday**			
Saturday			
Date : **Sunday**			

thinkpositive ● exercise daily
eat healthy ● dance more
Love often ● be happy

	Breakfast	Lunch	Dinner
Date : **Monday**			
Date : **Tuesday**			
Date : **Wednesday**			
Date : **Thursday**			
Date : **Friday**			
Saturday			
Date : **Sunday**			

thinkpositive ● exercise daily
eat healthy ●dance more
Love often● be happy

Notes:

Things
to Buy:

thinkpositive ● exercise daily
eat healthy ● dance more
Love often ● be happy

Meal Planner

Meal Planner

thinkpositive ● exercise daily
eat healthy ● dance more
Love often ● be happy

	Breakfast	Lunch	Dinner
Date : **Monday**			
Date : **Tuesday**			
Date : **Wednesday**			
Date : **Thursday**			
Date : **Friday**			
  Saturday			
Date : **Sunday**			

thinkpositive ● exercise daily
eat healthy ● dance more
Love often ● be happy

	Breakfast	Lunch	Dinner
Date : **Monday**			
Date : **Tuesday**			
Date : **Wednesday**			
Date : **Thursday**			
Date : **Friday**			
Saturday			
Date : **Sunday**			

thinkpositive ● exercise daily
eat healthy ● dance more
Love often ● be happy

	Breakfast	Lunch	Dinner
Date : **Monday**			
Date : **Tuesday**			
Date : **Wednesday**			
Date : **Thursday**			
Date : **Friday**			
Saturday			
Date : **Sunday**			

thinkpositive ● exercise daily
eat healthy ● dance more
Love often ● be happy

	Breakfast	Lunch	Dinner
Date : **Monday**			
Date : **Tuesday**			
Date : **Wednesday**			
Date : **Thursday**			
Date : **Friday**			
Saturday			
Date : **Sunday**			

thinkpositive ● exercise daily
eat healthy ● dance more
Love often ● be happy

Notes:

Things to Buy:

thinkpositive ● exercise daily
eat healthy ● dance more
Love often ● be happy

Meal Planner

Meal Planner

thinkpositive ● exercise daily
eat healthy ● dance more
Love often ● be happy

thinkpositive ● exercise daily
eat healthy ● dance more
Love often ● be happy

	Breakfast	Lunch	Dinner
Date : **Monday**			
Date : **Tuesday**			
Date : **Wednesday**			
Date : **Thursday**			
Date : **Friday**			
Saturday			
Date : **Sunday**			

thinkpositive ● exercise daily
eat healthy ● dance more
Love often ● be happy

	Breakfast	Lunch	Dinner
Date : **Monday**			
Date : **Tuesday**			
Date : **Wednesday**			
Date : **Thursday**			
Date : **Friday**			
Saturday			
Date : **Sunday**			

thinkpositive ● exercise daily
eat healthy ● dance more
Love often ● be happy

	Breakfast	Lunch	Dinner
Date : **Monday**			
Date : **Tuesday**			
Date : **Wednesday**			
Date : **Thursday**			
Date : **Friday**			
Saturday			
Date : **Sunday**			

thinkpositive ● exercise daily
eat healthy ● dance more
Love often ● be happy

	Breakfast	Lunch	Dinner
Date : **Monday**			
Date : **Tuesday**			
Date : **Wednesday**			
Date : **Thursday**			
Date : **Friday**			
Saturday			
Date : **Sunday**			

thinkpositive ● exercise daily
eat healthy ● dance more
Love often ● be happy

Notes:

Things to Buy:

thinkpositive ● exercise daily
eat healthy ● dance more
Love often ● be happy

thinkpositive ● exercise daily
eat healthy●dance more
Love often● be happy

Meal Planner

September

thinkpositive ● exercise daily
eat healthy ● dance more
Love often ● be happy

	Breakfast	Lunch	Dinner
Date : **Monday**			
Date : **Tuesday**			
Date : **Wednesday**			
Date : **Thursday**			
Date : **Friday**			
Saturday			
Date : **Sunday**			

thinkpositive ● exercise daily
eat healthy ● dance more
Love often ● be happy

	Breakfast	Lunch	Dinner
Date : **Monday**			
Date : **Tuesday**			
Date : **Wednesday**			
Date : **Thursday**			
Date : **Friday**			
Saturday			
Date : **Sunday**			

thinkpositive ● exercise daily
eat healthy ● dance more
Love often ● be happy

	Breakfast	Lunch	Dinner
Date : **Monday**			
Date : **Tuesday**			
Date : **Wednesday**			
Date : **Thursday**			
Date : **Friday**			
Saturday			
Date : **Sunday**			

thinkpositive ● exercise daily
eat healthy ● dance more
Love often ● be happy

	Breakfast	Lunch	Dinner
Date : **Monday**			
Date : **Tuesday**			
Date : **Wednesday**			
Date : **Thursday**			
Date : **Friday**			
Saturday			
Date : **Sunday**			

thinkpositive ● exercise daily
eat healthy ● dance more
Love often ● be happy

Notes:

Things to Buy:

thinkpositive ● exercise daily
eat healthy ● dance more
Love often ● be happy

Meal Planner

thinkpositive ● exercise daily
eat healthy● dance more
Love often● be happy

Meal Planner

October

thinkpositive ● exercise daily
eat healthy ● dance more
Love often ● be happy

	Breakfast	Lunch	Dinner
Date : **Monday**			
Date : **Tuesday**			
Date : **Wednesday**			
Date : **Thursday**			
Date : **Friday**			
  Saturday			
Date : **Sunday**			

thinkpositive ● exercise daily
eat healthy ● dance more
Love often ● be happy

	Breakfast	Lunch	Dinner
Date : **Monday**			
Date : **Tuesday**			
Date : **Wednesday**			
Date : **Thursday**			
Date : **Friday**			
Saturday			
Date : **Sunday**			

thinkpositive ● exercise daily
eat healthy ● dance more
Love often ● be happy

	Breakfast	Lunch	Dinner
Date : **Monday**			
Date : **Tuesday**			
Date : **Wednesday**			
Date : **Thursday**			
Date : **Friday**			
Saturday			
Date : **Sunday**			

thinkpositive ● exercise daily
eat healthy ● dance more
Love often ● be happy

	Breakfast	Lunch	Dinner
Date : **Monday**			
Date : **Tuesday**			
Date : **Wednesday**			
Date : **Thursday**			
Date : **Friday**			
Saturday			
Date : **Sunday**			

thinkpositive ● exercise daily
eat healthy ● dance more
Love often ● be happy

Notes:

Things to Buy:

thinkpositive ● exercise daily
eat healthy ● dance more
Love often ● be happy

Meal Planner

Meal Planner

thinkpositive ● exercise daily
eat healthy ● dance more
Love often ● be happy

thinkpositive ● exercise daily
eat healthy ● dance more
Love often ● be happy

	Breakfast	Lunch	Dinner
Date : **Monday**			
Date : **Tuesday**			
Date : **Wednesday**			
Date : **Thursday**			
Date : **Friday**			
Saturday			
Date : **Sunday**			

thinkpositive ● exercise daily
eat healthy ● dance more
Love often ● be happy

	Breakfast	Lunch	Dinner
Date : **Monday**			
Date : **Tuesday**			
Date : **Wednesday**			
Date : **Thursday**			
Date : **Friday**			
Saturday			
Date : **Sunday**			

thinkpositive ● exercise daily
eat healthy ● dance more
Love often ● be happy

	Breakfast	Lunch	Dinner
Date : **Monday**			
Date : **Tuesday**			
Date : **Wednesday**			
Date : **Thursday**			
Date : **Friday**			
Saturday			
Date : **Sunday**			

thinkpositive ● exercise daily
eat healthy ● dance more
Love often ● be happy

	Breakfast	Lunch	Dinner
Date : **Monday**			
Date : **Tuesday**			
Date : **Wednesday**			
Date : **Thursday**			
Date : **Friday**			
Saturday			
Date : **Sunday**			

thinkpositive ● exercise daily
eat healthy ● dance more
Love often ● be happy

Notes:

Things to Buy:

thinkpositive ● exercise daily
eat healthy ● dance more
Love often ● be happy

Meal Planner

thinkpositive ● exercise daily
eat healthy ● dance more
Love often ● be happy

thinkpositive ● exercise daily
eat healthy ● dance more
Love often ● be happy

thinkpositive ● exercise daily
eat healthy ● dance more
Love often ● be happy

	Breakfast	Lunch	Dinner
Date : **Monday**			
Date : **Tuesday**			
Date : **Wednesday**			
Date : **Thursday**			
Date : **Friday**			
Saturday			
Date : **Sunday**			

thinkpositive ● exercise daily
eat healthy ● dance more
Love often ● be happy

	Breakfast	Lunch	Dinner
Date : **Monday**			
Date : **Tuesday**			
Date : **Wednesday**			
Date : **Thursday**			
Date : **Friday**			
Saturday			
Date : **Sunday**			

thinkpositive ● exercise daily
eat healthy ● dance more
Love often ● be happy

	Breakfast	Lunch	Dinner
Date : **Monday**			
Date : **Tuesday**			
Date : **Wednesday**			
Date : **Thursday**			
Date : **Friday**			
Saturday			
Date : **Sunday**			

thinkpositive ● exercise daily
eat healthy ● dance more
Love often ● be happy

	Breakfast	Lunch	Dinner
Date : **Monday**			
Date : **Tuesday**			
Date : **Wednesday**			
Date : **Thursday**			
Date : **Friday**			
Saturday			
Date : **Sunday**			

thinkpositive ● exercise daily
eat healthy ● dance more
Love often ● be happy

Notes:

Things
to Buy:

thinkpositive ● exercise daily
eat healthy ● dance more
Love often ● be happy

Meal Planner

thinkpositive ● exercise daily
eat healthy ● dance more
Love often ● be happy

Meal Planner

thinkpositive ● exercise daily
eat healthy ● dance more
Love often ● be happy

	Breakfast	Lunch	Dinner
Date : **Monday**			
Date : **Tuesday**			
Date : **Wednesday**			
Date : **Thursday**			
Date : **Friday**			
Saturday			
Date : **Sunday**			

thinkpositive ● exercise daily
eat healthy ● dance more
Love often ● be happy

	Breakfast	Lunch	Dinner
Date : **Monday**			
Date : **Tuesday**			
Date : **Wednesday**			
Date : **Thursday**			
Date : **Friday**			
Saturday			
Date : **Sunday**			

thinkpositive ● exercise daily
eat healthy ● dance more
Love often ● be happy

	Breakfast	Lunch	Dinner
Date : **Monday**			
Date : **Tuesday**			
Date : **Wednesday**			
Date : **Thursday**			
Date : **Friday**			
Saturday			
Date : **Sunday**			

thinkpositive ● exercise daily
eat healthy ● dance more
Love often ● be happy

	Breakfast	Lunch	Dinner
Date : **Monday**			
Date : **Tuesday**			
Date : **Wednesday**			
Date : **Thursday**			
Date : **Friday**			
Saturday			
Date : **Sunday**			

thinkpositive ● exercise daily
eat healthy ● dance more
Love often ● be happy

	Breakfast	Lunch	Dinner
Date : **Monday**			
Date : **Tuesday**			
Date : **Wednesday**			
Date : **Thursday**			
Date : **Friday**			
Saturday			
Date : **Sunday**			

thinkpositive ● exercise daily
eat healthy ● dance more
Love often ● be happy

	Breakfast	Lunch	Dinner
Date : **Monday**			
Date : **Tuesday**			
Date : **Wednesday**			
Date : **Thursday**			
Date : **Friday**			
Saturday			
Date : **Sunday**			

thinkpositive ● exercise daily
eat healthy ● dance more
Love often ● be happy

	Breakfast	Lunch	Dinner
Date : **Monday**			
Date : **Tuesday**			
Date : **Wednesday**			
Date : **Thursday**			
Date : **Friday**			
Saturday			
Date : **Sunday**			

thinkpositive ● exercise daily
eat healthy ●dance more
Love often● be happy

	Breakfast	Lunch	Dinner
Date : **Monday**			
Date : **Tuesday**			
Date : **Wednesday**			
Date : **Thursday**			
Date : **Friday**			
Saturday			
Date : **Sunday**			

thinkpositive ● exercise daily
eat healthy ● dance more
Love often ● be happy